Ghosts of Oregon: The Top 10 Haunted Places You Must Visit

Ghosts of Oregon: The Top 10 Haunted Places You Must Visit

Edward Turner

Published by Oliver Lancaster, 2023.

While every precaution has been taken in the preparation of this book, the publisher assumes no responsibility for errors or omissions, or for damages resulting from the use of the information contained herein.

GHOSTS OF OREGON: THE TOP 10 HAUNTED PLACES YOU MUST VISIT

First edition. July 8, 2023.

ISBN: 979-8223280569

Written by Edward Turner.

Also by Edward Turner

Ghosts of Paris: Ten Haunted Places in the City of Love
Appalachian Nightmares: The Top 10 Creepy Creatures of the Mountains
Asia's Top Ten Cryptids: Legends, Sightings, and Theories
Beyond the Shadows: Unlocking the Mystery of Bigfoot
Evil Women in History: Uncovering the Gruesome Crimes of Ten Notorious Female Killers
Ghosts of London: Ten Haunted Places in The City
Ghosts of New York: Ten Haunted Places in The Big Apple
Ghosts of Oregon: The Top 10 Haunted Places You Must Visit
Ghosts of the Stage: Ten Hauntings at the Theatre
Missouri Nightmares: The Top 10 Chilling Legends
Mothman Unleashed: Into the Darkened Skies
North America's Top Ten Cryptids: Legends, Sightings, and Theories
Philly's Phantom Encounters: Exploring the City's Most Haunted Places
Secrets of the Deep: The Mystery of the Loch Ness Monster
Unsolved Mysteries: Delving into the Shadows of Infamous Murders and Enigmatic Killers
Unveiling the Shadows: A Journey into Financial Crimes and Scandals

Introduction

History of Oregon's paranormal history

Oregon is a state with a rich and fascinating paranormal history. From ghost sightings to unexplained phenomena, the state is home to numerous haunted locations that continue to intrigue and fascinate visitors and locals alike. The origins of Oregon's paranormal history can be traced back to its early history, with many tales of hauntings and ghostly encounters dating back to the 19th century.

One of the most famous tales of Oregon's paranormal history involves the Shanghai Tunnels. These tunnels, located beneath Portland's Old Town, were used during the late 19th and early 20th centuries to transport goods and people from the waterfront to the city's downtown area. However, they were also used by criminal gangs to kidnap unsuspecting victims and sell them into forced labour on ships bound for Asia. Legend has it that the ghosts of these victims still haunt the tunnels to this day, with many visitors reporting eerie sounds and sightings of ghostly apparitions.

Another famous haunted location in Oregon is the Oregon State Hospital. Originally known as the Oregon State Insane Asylum, this hospital was established in the late 19th century to house mentally ill patients. However, over the years, it became notorious for its inhuman treatment of patients, with reports of electroshock therapy and lobotomies being performed on patients without their consent. Many believe that the ghosts of these mistreated patients still haunt the hospital, with numerous sightings of ghostly apparitions and unexplained sounds and smells reported by staff and visitors alike.

The McMenamins White Eagle Saloon is another location that is steeped in Oregon's paranormal history. This saloon, located in Portland's industrial district, was established in 1905 and quickly became a popular spot for dockworkers and loggers. However, it was also notorious for its rough and rowdy atmosphere, with many fights and brawls breaking out among patrons. Legend has it that the ghosts of these rowdy patrons still haunt the saloon to this day, with many visitors reporting sightings of ghostly apparitions and unexplained sounds and smells.

The Heceta Head Lighthouse, located on the Oregon coast, is another location with a long and fascinating paranormal history. Built in 1894, this lighthouse is considered one of the most haunted locations in the state, with numerous reports of ghostly apparitions and unexplained sounds and smells. Legend has it that the ghost of a woman named Rue still haunts the lighthouse to this day, with many visitors reporting sightings of her ghostly figure.

Oregon's paranormal history is not just limited to haunted buildings and locations, however. The state is also home to numerous unexplained phenomena, such as the famous Oregon Vortex. Located near Gold Hill, this mysterious site is known for its strange gravitational anomalies and optical illusions. Visitors to the Oregon Vortex report feeling disoriented and dizzy, and objects placed on the site appear to roll uphill instead of down.

Oregon's paranormal history is a rich and fascinating tapestry of ghost stories, haunted locations, and unexplained phenomena. From the Shanghai Tunnels to the Heceta Head Lighthouse, the state is home to numerous haunted locations that continue to intrigue and fascinate visitors and locals alike. Whether you believe in ghosts and the paranormal or not, there is no denying the allure and mystique of Oregon's haunted history.

Chapter 1: The Shanghai Tunnels

History of the tunnels and their original purpose

The Shanghai Tunnels, located beneath the streets of Old Town Portland, Oregon, have a dark and fascinating history. Originally constructed in the 1850s, these underground tunnels were used for a variety of purposes, including transporting goods, providing access to basements, and housing Chinese immigrants who were forcibly kidnapped and sold into servitude.

The tunnels were initially built to provide easy access to the waterfront, which was the heart of commerce in Portland during the 19th century. However, as the city grew, the tunnels took on a new purpose as a means of transporting goods from the waterfront to businesses located further inland. The tunnels were used by businesses to store and transport their goods, and they also provided easy access to basements, which were used for storage and as living quarters for workers.

However, it was not long before the tunnels began to be used for more sinister purposes. Portland had a large population of Chinese immigrants who had come to work on the railroads and in the mines. These immigrants were often subjected to discrimination and violence, and many were kidnapped and sold into servitude by "crimps" who operated in the city's underground world. These crimps would capture unsuspecting Chinese immigrants and hold them captive in the tunnels until they could be sold to ship captains who needed labourers for their journeys to Asia.

The conditions in the tunnels were appalling. Chinese immigrants were held in small, cramped cells and subjected to brutal treatment. They were often beaten and starved, and many died in the tunnels due to the inhumane conditions. Some estimates suggest that as many as 1,000 Chinese immigrants were kidnapped and sold into servitude in the Portland area between 1850 and 1941.

In addition to the kidnapping and sale of Chinese immigrants, the Shanghai Tunnels were also used for a variety of illegal activities, including gambling and prostitution. The tunnels were a popular location for these activities because they provided a degree of privacy and anonymity.

Today, the Shanghai Tunnels are a popular tourist attraction, and visitors can take guided tours of the underground tunnels to learn more about their history. The tunnels have been extensively restored and renovated, and many of the original artefacts and structures can still be seen today. However, the dark history of the tunnels remains a haunting reminder of Portland's past, and serves as a reminder of the inhumanity and injustice that occurred in the city's underground world.

Stories of kidnapping and forced labour

THE HISTORY OF KIDNAPPING and forced labour in the Portland area is a dark chapter in the city's history. The practice was primarily aimed at Chinese immigrants who had come to the area to work in the mines or on the railroads, and who were often subjected to discrimination and violence.

The practice of kidnapping Chinese immigrants and selling them into servitude was known as "shanghaiing," and it was a common occurrence in the late 19th and early 20th centuries. Many of these kidnappings occurred in the city's underground world, which included the infamous Shanghai Tunnels.

One of the most well-known stories of shanghaiing in Portland involves a man named Jim Turk, who was a notorious crimp and kidnapper in the city. Turk was known for his brutal methods, and he was responsible for kidnapping and selling hundreds of Chinese immigrants into servitude.

Turk's most famous victim was a man named "One-Eyed" Jimmie. Jimmie was a Chinese immigrant who was kidnapped by Turk and held captive in the Shanghai Tunnels. He was eventually sold to a ship captain who was travelling to Asia, and he spent several years working as a labourer before he was able to escape and make his way back to Portland.

Another well-known victim of shanghaiing in Portland was a man named Joe Bodie. Bodie was a Chinese immigrant who was kidnapped and sold into servitude by a crimp named Johnny Wong. Bodie spent several years working on a ship before he was able to escape and return to Portland, where he worked to expose the practice of shanghaiing and bring the crimps to justice.

The practice of shanghaiing was not limited to Chinese immigrants, however. Other groups, such as sailors and other transient workers, were also targeted by the crimps. In fact, it is estimated that as many as 2,000 men were shanghaied in Portland between 1875 and 1910.

Today, the stories of kidnapping and forced labour in Portland serve as a reminder of the city's troubled past. Many of the victims of shanghaiing were subjected to inhumane conditions and brutal treatment, and their stories serve as a haunting reminder of the injustice and cruelty that occurred in the city's underground world. While the practice of shanghaiing is no longer a threat in modern-day Portland, the stories of those who suffered under this practice continue to be an important part of the city's history.

Paranormal activity reported in the tunnels

THE SHANGHAI TUNNELS, located beneath the streets of Portland, Oregon, are famous for their dark history and the paranormal activity that has been reported within their walls. The tunnels were originally built in the mid-19th century to transport goods and people from the docks along the Willamette River to the city's downtown area. However, the tunnels became notorious for their use in the practice of "shanghaiing," in which unsuspecting men were kidnapped and sold into forced labour on ships.

GHOSTS OF OREGON: THE TOP 10 HAUNTED PLACES YOU MUST VISIT

Today, many visitors to the Shanghai Tunnels report experiencing strange sensations and unexplained events that they attribute to paranormal activity. One of the most commonly reported phenomena is the feeling of being watched or followed. Visitors have reported feeling as though someone is walking behind them or even grabbing their clothing, only to turn around and find no one there.

Other visitors to the tunnels have reported hearing disembodied voices, footsteps, and other unexplained sounds. Some have even reported hearing the sounds of chains and shackles, as though the ghosts of the shanghaied men are still trapped within the tunnels.

There have also been numerous reports of apparitions and shadow figures in the Shanghai Tunnels. Visitors have reported seeing figures walking through the tunnels, only to disappear when they get closer. Others have reported seeing ghostly figures standing in doorways or peering out from behind corners.

Perhaps the most famous ghost associated with the Shanghai Tunnels is that of Nina, a prostitute who was said to have been kidnapped and forced to work in the tunnels. Visitors have reported seeing Nina's ghost in the tunnels, as well as hearing her voice and feeling her presence.

In addition to these paranormal experiences, there have also been reports of more physical manifestations of paranormal activity in the Shanghai Tunnels. Visitors have reported feeling sudden drops in temperature, as well as feeling physical sensations such as being touched or pushed.

Despite the numerous reports of paranormal activity in the Shanghai Tunnels, sceptics point out that many of these experiences could be explained by more mundane causes, such as drafts and natural phenomena. However, for those who believe in ghosts and the paranormal, the Shanghai Tunnels remain a fascinating and eerie destination, filled with the ghosts of Portland's troubled past.

Chapter 2: The McMenamins White Eagle Saloon

The history of the saloon and its significance

The McMenamins White Eagle Saloon is a historic bar located in the heart of Portland, Oregon. The building that houses the bar was originally constructed in 1905 and has a rich and varied history that is closely tied to the development of the city itself.

The saloon was originally established by a Polish immigrant named W.R. Wilklow, who wanted to create a gathering place for his fellow immigrants. The bar quickly became a popular destination for Portland's working class, who would come to the White Eagle to socialise, drink, and enjoy live music.

Over the years, the White Eagle became known for its raucous atmosphere and wild parties. It was a popular destination for loggers, sailors, and other rough and tumble characters who were drawn to the bar's lively energy and strong drinks.

During Prohibition, the White Eagle continued to operate as a speakeasy, serving illegal alcohol to thirsty patrons. It was during this time that the bar gained a reputation for being a centre of illicit activity and a hub for Portland's underworld.

In the decades that followed, the White Eagle underwent several changes in ownership and fell into disrepair. However, in the 1990s, it was purchased by the McMenamins brewery chain, which set about restoring the bar to its former glory.

Today, the White Eagle Saloon is a beloved institution in Portland and a popular destination for locals and tourists alike. The bar has been restored to its original splendour, with vintage decor and memorabilia adorning the walls and ceilings.

One of the most significant aspects of the White Eagle's history is its connection to Portland's Polish immigrant community. The bar was established at a time when Polish immigrants were flocking to the city in search of work and a better life. The White Eagle served as a gathering place for these immigrants, providing them with a sense of community and belonging in a new and unfamiliar city.

In addition to its cultural significance, the White Eagle has also played an important role in the development of Portland's music scene. The bar has hosted countless live music performances over the years, featuring a wide range of local and national acts. Many of these performances have helped to launch the careers of up-and-coming musicians and have contributed to the vibrant music scene that exists in Portland today.

Despite its long and storied history, the White Eagle Saloon remains a vital and active part of Portland's social and cultural landscape. Its significance as a gathering place for Portland's working class, its connection to the city's Polish immigrant community, and its role in the development of Portland's music scene have made it an important cultural institution and a beloved destination for generations of Portlanders.

Stories of the saloon's past patrons and employees

AS ONE OF THE OLDEST bars in Portland, the McMenamins White Eagle Saloon has seen its fair share of colourful characters over the years. From loggers and sailors to musicians and artists, the White Eagle has always been a gathering place for a diverse and eclectic crowd.

One of the most famous stories associated with the White Eagle involves a former employee named Sam Warrick. Warrick worked at the bar during the 1920s and 30s and was known for his quick wit and sharp tongue. Legend has it that he would often play practical jokes on patrons and was known to pour water down the backs of unsuspecting customers.

Another well-known figure from the White Eagle's past is a man named Mickey O'Brien. O'Brien was a regular at the bar during the 1940s and 50s and was known for his fiery temper and brawling nature. He was also an accomplished boxer and would often challenge other patrons to fights in the bar's back room.

In addition to its colourful patrons, the White Eagle has also been home to a number of interesting employees over the years. One such employee was a woman named Rose, who worked at the bar in the 1920s and 30s. Rose was a tough and no-nonsense bartender who was known for her ability to handle even the rowdiest of customers.

Another well-known employee from the White Eagle's past is a man named Tom McCall. McCall worked at the bar during the 1940s and 50s and went on to become the governor of Oregon in the 1960s and 70s. McCall was known for his love of the White Eagle and would often talk about his time working at the bar during his political speeches.

Over the years, the White Eagle has also been a popular destination for musicians and artists. The bar has hosted countless live music performances over the years, featuring a wide range of local and national acts. One of the most famous musicians to play at the White Eagle was a man named Woody Guthrie, who performed at the bar in the 1940s.

Despite its colourful and sometimes rowdy history, the White Eagle has always been a beloved institution in Portland. Its connection to the city's working class, its role in the development of Portland's music scene, and its long and storied history have made it an important cultural institution and a beloved destination for generations of Portlanders.

Today, the White Eagle continues to thrive as a popular bar and music venue, hosting live performances and serving up cold drinks to a new generation of patrons. Its colourful past and rich history have cemented its place in the hearts and minds of Portlanders, making it a beloved and iconic institution in the city's cultural landscape.

Paranormal activity reported in the saloon

THE MCMENAMINS WHITE Eagle Saloon is not just a popular bar and music venue in Portland, it is also widely known for its reported paranormal activity. Over the years, many patrons and employees have reported experiencing strange occurrences and eerie sensations while inside the bar, leading some to believe that the White Eagle is haunted.

One of the most common reports of paranormal activity at the White Eagle involves the presence of ghostly apparitions. Many people have reported seeing shadowy figures and ghostly shapes moving about the bar, especially in the back room and upstairs areas. Some have even reported seeing full-bodied apparitions of former patrons and employees, including the ghost of a former bartender named Rose.

Another common report of paranormal activity at the White Eagle involves unexplained sounds and voices. Many people have reported hearing strange noises, such as footsteps, doors opening and closing, and even whispers and voices that seem to come from nowhere. Some have even reported hearing the sounds of old-time music playing, even when there is no music playing in the bar.

In addition to these sightings and sounds, there have also been reports of objects moving on their own and other strange phenomena. Glasses have been known to move and tip over by themselves, while chairs and other objects have been reported to move on their own, seemingly without any explanation. Some people have also reported feeling cold spots or sudden drops in temperature, even on warm days.

The stories of paranormal activity at the White Eagle date back decades, and many of the reports involve the presence of ghostly figures and strange occurrences in the bar's upstairs area. In fact, many people believe that the upstairs area is the most haunted part of the bar, with reports of ghostly activity dating back to the early 1900s.

One of the most famous stories associated with the White Eagle's upstairs area involves the ghost of a woman who is said to have died in the building many years ago. According to the story, the woman was murdered by her husband and her body was hidden in one of the upstairs rooms. To this day, many people claim to have seen her ghostly figure wandering through the upstairs area of the bar.

Another common report of paranormal activity at the White Eagle involves the presence of a ghostly figure known as "Sammy." According to legend, Sammy was a former employee of the bar who died in the building many years ago. His ghostly figure has been seen by many people over the years, and some claim that he is responsible for the strange occurrences that happen in the bar.

Despite the reports of paranormal activity, the White Eagle remains a popular destination for Portlanders and visitors alike. Many people are drawn to the bar because of its rich history and cultural significance, while others come in search of a glimpse of the paranormal activity that has been reported over the years.

GHOSTS OF OREGON: THE TOP 10 HAUNTED PLACES YOU MUST VISIT

Whether you believe in ghosts or not, there is no denying that the White Eagle Saloon is a unique and fascinating place with a history that is deeply intertwined with the city of Portland.

Chapter 3: Geiser Grand Hotel

The history of the hotel and the Gold Rush

The Geiser Grand Hotel is a historic hotel located in Baker City, Oregon. The hotel was originally built in 1889 by Augustus Geiser, a prominent businessman who made his fortune in the Gold Rush. The Geiser Grand Hotel quickly became a popular destination for travellers and miners alike, thanks to its luxurious accommodations and prime location in the heart of Baker City.

The Geiser Grand Hotel was designed by architect John Bennes, who was known for his elegant and ornate designs. Bennes incorporated elements of Victorian and Art Nouveau styles into the hotel's design, creating a stunning building that was both beautiful and functional.

In addition to its luxurious accommodations, the Geiser Grand Hotel was also known for its state-of-the-art amenities, which included electric lights, steam heat, and hot and cold running water. These amenities were virtually unheard of in the late 1800s, and the Geiser Grand Hotel quickly became a symbol of luxury and sophistication in the Pacific Northwest.

The hotel's connection to the Gold Rush was also an important factor in its success. Baker City was a major centre of mining activity in the late 1800s, and the Geiser Grand Hotel provided a comfortable and convenient place for miners to stay while they worked in the nearby mines. The hotel also played an important role in the social and cultural life of the town, hosting balls, parties, and other events that were attended by both locals and visitors.

Despite its early success, the Geiser Grand Hotel fell into decline in the early 1900s. The Gold Rush had come to an end, and Baker City's economy had shifted away from mining and toward agriculture and other industries. The hotel changed hands several times over the years, and by the 1960s it had fallen into disrepair and was in danger of being demolished.

In the 1970s, a group of local investors purchased the Geiser Grand Hotel and began a painstaking restoration process. The hotel was restored to its former glory, with much of the original decor and furnishings being salvaged and restored. Today, the Geiser Grand Hotel is a popular destination for tourists and history buffs alike, offering a glimpse into the past and the rich history of Baker City and the Pacific Northwest.

In addition to its historical significance, the Geiser Grand Hotel is also known for its reported paranormal activity. Over the years, many guests and employees have reported experiencing strange occurrences and eerie sensations while inside the hotel, leading some to believe that the Geiser Grand is haunted by the ghosts of former guests and employees.

Despite the reports of paranormal activity, the Geiser Grand Hotel remains a popular destination for travellers from around the world. Its rich history, elegant design, and connection to the

Gold Rush make it a fascinating and unique destination that is sure to appeal to anyone with an interest in history and culture.

Stories of past guests and employees

AS ONE OF THE OLDEST and most historic hotels in the Pacific Northwest, the Geiser Grand Hotel has seen its fair share of guests and employees over the years. Many of these people have reported strange and unexplained occurrences during their stay at the hotel, leading some to believe that the Geiser Grand is haunted by the ghosts of its past.

One of the most famous stories about the Geiser Grand Hotel involves a former guest who stayed in Room 302, which is said to be one of the most haunted rooms in the hotel. According to the story, the guest was awakened in the middle of the night by a strange noise coming from the corner of the room. When he turned on the light, he saw the ghostly figure of a woman standing in the corner, staring at him with cold, unseeing eyes. The guest was so frightened by the experience that he immediately checked out of the hotel and never returned.

Another famous story involves a former employee who worked as a housekeeper at the Geiser Grand Hotel. According to the employee, she often heard strange noises and voices while cleaning the hotel rooms late at night. One night, while cleaning Room 202, the employee heard a loud banging noise coming from the closet. When she opened the closet door, she saw the ghostly figure of a man hanging from a rope. The employee was so terrified by the experience that she quit her job at the hotel the next day.

Other stories involve strange smells, cold spots, and unexplained footsteps heard throughout the hotel. Some guests have reported seeing ghostly apparitions in the hallways, while others have reported feeling an eerie presence in their rooms. Despite the many reports of paranormal activity, the owners and employees of the Geiser Grand Hotel remain sceptical, and there has been no scientific evidence to support the claims of ghostly activity in the hotel.

Despite the scepticism, many visitors to the Geiser Grand Hotel are drawn to its rich history and haunted reputation. The hotel offers guided ghost tours that take guests through the most haunted areas of the building, providing a glimpse into the past and the mysterious world of the paranormal. Whether you believe in ghosts or not, the Geiser Grand Hotel remains one of the most fascinating and historic destinations in the Pacific Northwest, offering a unique and unforgettable experience for anyone with an interest in history, culture, and the unexplained.

Paranormal activity reported in the hotel

THE GEISER GRAND HOTEL is known for its rich history and stunning architecture, but it is also notorious for its reported paranormal activity. Guests and staff members alike have reported strange occurrences, ghostly apparitions, and unexplained phenomena throughout the hotel, leading many to believe that the Geiser Grand is haunted by the ghosts of its past.

One of the most commonly reported incidents at the Geiser Grand is the sighting of ghostly figures in various parts of the hotel. Some guests have reported seeing apparitions dressed in period clothing, while others have reported seeing shadowy figures moving through the hallways or standing in doorways. One guest even reported seeing a ghostly woman sitting in a chair in the lobby, watching him intently before disappearing into thin air.

Another common occurrence at the Geiser Grand is unexplained noises and sounds. Guests have reported hearing footsteps in empty hallways, knocking on doors with no one on the other side, and even voices whispering in their ears. One guest reported hearing the sound of a woman crying in her room, even though there was no one else in the room with her.

Cold spots and sudden drops in temperature have also been reported at the Geiser Grand. Some guests have reported feeling a sudden chill in certain areas of the hotel, despite the fact that the temperature was normal in other parts of the building. Some have also reported feeling a presence in their room or a feeling of being watched, accompanied by a sudden drop in temperature.

One of the most notorious incidents at the Geiser Grand involves the haunted Room 302. Guests who have stayed in this room have reported a variety of strange occurrences, including the feeling of being watched, objects moving on their own, and even the ghostly figure of a woman standing in the corner of the room. Some guests have even reported waking up in the middle of the night to find the ghostly figure of a woman sitting on the edge of their bed.

Despite the many reports of paranormal activity at the Geiser Grand, there has been no scientific evidence to support the claims of ghostly activity in the hotel. The owners and staff members of the hotel remain sceptical, attributing the reports to the hotel's rich history and the power of suggestion.

However, for those who believe in the paranormal, the Geiser Grand Hotel offers a unique and unforgettable experience. The hotel offers guided ghost tours that take visitors through the most haunted areas of the building, providing a glimpse into the past and the mysterious world of the paranormal. Whether you believe in ghosts or not, the Geiser Grand Hotel remains a fascinating and historic destination, offering a glimpse into the unknown and the unexplained.

Chapter 4: The Oregon State Hospital

The history of the hospital and its treatment of patients

The Oregon State Hospital, located in Salem, has a long and often controversial history. Originally known as the Oregon State Insane Asylum, it was established in 1883 to provide care and treatment for individuals with mental illnesses. The hospital was intended to be a modern and humane facility, but its treatment of patients was often anything but.

In the early days of the hospital, patients were often treated with crude and inhumane methods. They were confined to cramped and overcrowded wards, subjected to forced labour, and treated with harsh medications and electroshock therapy. Patients who were deemed difficult or unmanageable were often subjected to solitary confinement, which could last for weeks or even months.

One of the most notorious periods in the hospital's history occurred in the 1940s and 1950s, when the hospital was the subject of a scandal involving the mistreatment of patients. The hospital was overcrowded, understaffed, and plagued by unsanitary conditions. Patients were subjected to shock treatments, lobotomies, and other forms of medical experimentation, often without their consent. The scandal led to reforms in the hospital's treatment of patients and increased scrutiny of the treatment of mental illness in the United States.

In the 1970s, the hospital underwent significant changes, with a focus on improving patient care and increasing community involvement in mental health treatment. The hospital implemented new programs to provide more humane and effective treatment for patients, including art therapy, music therapy, and occupational therapy. Patients were given more autonomy and were encouraged to participate in their own treatment plans.

Today, the Oregon State Hospital continues to provide care and treatment for individuals with mental illnesses. The hospital has undergone significant renovations and upgrades in recent years, with a focus on providing a safe and comfortable environment for patients. The hospital's treatment methods have also evolved, with a focus on evidence-based practices and a patient-centred approach to care.

Despite its troubled history, the Oregon State Hospital remains an important institution in the treatment of mental illness in the United States. Its legacy serves as a reminder of the need for humane and effective treatment of individuals with mental illnesses, and the ongoing importance of addressing the stigma surrounding mental health issues.

Stories of past patients and staff

OVER THE YEARS, THE Oregon State Hospital has been home to thousands of patients and staff members. Some of these individuals have left a lasting mark on the hospital's history, with stories of their lives and experiences still echoing through the halls today.

One of the most famous former patients of the hospital is Ken Kesey, the author of "One Flew Over the Cuckoo's Nest." Kesey spent time at the hospital in the 1960s as part of an experimental drug study, which inspired his famous novel. While at the hospital, Kesey observed and interacted with other patients and staff members, many of whom served as inspiration for the characters in his book.

Another notable patient was Jack Beatty, who was admitted to the hospital in the 1920s after he was diagnosed with dementia praecox, a now-obsolete term for schizophrenia. Beatty spent over 20 years at the hospital, during which time he wrote extensively about his experiences. His writings provide a unique perspective on life at the hospital during the early part of the 20th century.

The hospital has also been home to many dedicated staff members over the years. One such individual was Dr. Dean Brooks, who served as the hospital's superintendent from 1955 to 1981. During his tenure, Brooks worked to reform the hospital's treatment methods and improve the lives of patients. He also had a significant impact on popular culture, thanks to his role in the filming of "One Flew Over the Cuckoo's Nest." Brooks played the character of Dr. Spivey in the movie and served as a consultant to the filmmakers.

Another notable staff member was Dr. J. Allen Boone, who served as the hospital's chief medical officer in the 1940s and 1950s. Boone was a pioneer in the field of occupational therapy, and his work at the hospital helped to establish the practice as a key part of mental health treatment. Boone also wrote extensively about his experiences at the hospital, providing a valuable glimpse into life at the facility during a tumultuous period in its history.

Of course, not all of the stories associated with the Oregon State Hospital are positive. The hospital's troubled history is filled with tales of mistreatment, abuse, and neglect. For many patients, the hospital was a place of suffering and despair, and their stories serve as a reminder of the need for compassionate and effective treatment of mental illness.

Despite its chequered past, the Oregon State Hospital remains an important institution in the treatment of mental illness. The stories of its past patients and staff members provide a unique perspective on the hospital's history, and serve as a reminder of the challenges and triumphs associated with caring for individuals with mental illnesses.

Paranormal activity reported in the hospital

THE OREGON STATE HOSPITAL is known not only for its treatment of mental illness but also for its alleged paranormal activity. Over the years, numerous reports have been made of unexplained phenomena and ghostly encounters within the hospital's walls.

One of the most famous stories associated with the hospital is that of the "phantom piper." According to legend, a former patient of the hospital was an accomplished bagpiper who played his instrument throughout the halls of the hospital. After his death, staff and patients reported hearing the sound of bagpipes echoing through the halls, even though no one was playing them.

Another reported paranormal occurrence is the appearance of "shadow people." Many individuals have reported seeing dark, shadowy figures moving through the hospital, often disappearing when approached. Some have speculated that these shadow figures could be the spirits of former patients, lingering in the hospital even after their deaths.

There have also been reports of apparitions, with some individuals claiming to have seen the ghostly forms of former patients or staff members. One of the most commonly reported apparitions is that of a nurse who allegedly haunts the hospital's underground tunnels. According to legend, the nurse died in the tunnels while trying to rescue patients during a fire, and her spirit has remained there ever since.

Another common ghostly sighting is that of a man in a suit and fedora hat, who has been spotted walking through the hospital's main lobby. Some speculate that this could be the spirit of a former administrator or patient who is still attached to the hospital in death.

In addition to these more specific reports, many individuals have reported a general feeling of unease or a sense of being watched while in the hospital. Others have claimed to hear unexplained noises, such as footsteps or voices, when no one else is present.

While there is no scientific proof of paranormal activity at the Oregon State Hospital, these reports have captured the imaginations of many people and have helped to cement the hospital's place in popular culture. Whether or not there are actually ghosts roaming the halls, the hospital's reputation as a haunted location adds an extra layer of intrigue to its already complex history.

Chapter 5: The Heceta Head Lighthouse

The history of the lighthouse

The Heceta Head Lighthouse is a historic lighthouse located on the coast of Oregon, about 13 miles north of Florence. First lit in 1894, it is one of the most iconic landmarks on the Oregon coast and is renowned for its unique architecture and stunning coastal views.

The lighthouse was named after Don Bruno de Heceta, a Spanish explorer who sailed along the Pacific coast in 1775. The site of the lighthouse was chosen due to the treacherous nature of the coastline, which had claimed the lives of many sailors over the years. The lighthouse was built to provide a beacon of light to guide ships safely through the dangerous waters.

Construction of the lighthouse began in 1892 and was completed two years later. The lighthouse was built using locally quarried stone and features a distinctive, octagonal shape. At the top of the lighthouse is a Fresnel lens, which was imported from France and is still in use today.

For many years, the lighthouse was operated by a team of lighthouse keepers, who were responsible for maintaining the light and ensuring that it remained in working order. Life at the lighthouse was often lonely and isolating, as the keepers were required to live on-site and were only allowed to leave the property once a month.

Despite the challenges of life at the lighthouse, many keepers found the experience to be rewarding. They were able to witness the beauty of the coast firsthand, and many developed a deep appreciation for the natural environment. Over the years, the lighthouse became a beloved symbol of the Oregon coast, attracting visitors from all over the world.

In 1963, the lighthouse was automated, and the need for full-time keepers was eliminated. Today, the Heceta Head Lighthouse is still in operation and is maintained by the U.S. Coast Guard. It is also a popular tourist destination, attracting visitors who come to admire the stunning views and learn about the history of the lighthouse and its keepers.

In addition to its historical significance, the Heceta Head Lighthouse is also known for its alleged paranormal activity. Over the years, many visitors and staff members have reported seeing ghostly apparitions and experiencing unexplained phenomena at the lighthouse. Some have even claimed to hear the voices of former keepers, as if they are still carrying out their duties in the afterlife.

Despite the reported paranormal activity, the Heceta Head Lighthouse remains a beloved symbol of the Oregon coast, and its rich history and stunning views continue to attract visitors from all over the world.

Stories of past keepers and their families

OVER THE YEARS, MANY keepers and their families have lived at the Heceta Head Lighthouse. Life at the lighthouse was often difficult and isolating, but many keepers found the experience to be rewarding, and they formed close-knit communities with their fellow keepers and their families.

One of the most famous keepers at the Heceta Head Lighthouse was Joshua Green, who served from 1894 to 1902. Green was known for his strict adherence to duty and his commitment to keeping the light burning brightly, even in the most challenging weather conditions. He was also known for his love of animals, and he kept several pets at the lighthouse, including a goat named Nanny.

Another famous keeper was James Gibbons, who served from 1902 to 1906. Gibbons was known for his love of music, and he often played his violin for his fellow keepers and their families. He was also an avid gardener and spent much of his free time tending to the lighthouse's gardens.

One of the most tragic stories of the Heceta Head Lighthouse involves a keeper named Frank Steinbach, who served from 1921 to 1925. Steinbach was married and had two young children, and he was known for his kind and gentle nature. However, he suffered from bouts of depression, which were exacerbated by the isolation and loneliness of life at the lighthouse.

In 1925, Steinbach's depression became too much to bear, and he took his own life by jumping from the cliffs near the lighthouse. His wife and children were devastated by his death, and they soon left the lighthouse to start a new life elsewhere. Today, many visitors to the lighthouse claim to have seen the ghostly apparition of a man walking along the cliffs, and some believe that it is the ghost of Frank Steinbach.

Another tragic story involves a keeper named Fred LaDue, who served from 1936 to 1940. LaDue was a heavy drinker, and his drinking often led to violent outbursts. One night, he got into a fight with his wife and began firing his gun, narrowly missing her and their two children. The next day, LaDue turned himself in to the authorities and was sentenced to prison. His wife and children left the lighthouse soon after, and LaDue was never able to return to his job as a lighthouse keeper.

Despite the challenges and tragedies that occurred at the Heceta Head Lighthouse over the years, many keepers and their families found joy and meaning in their work. They were able to witness the beauty of the Oregon coast firsthand, and they formed close bonds with their fellow keepers and their families. Today, the stories of these keepers and their families serve as a reminder of the rich history and heritage of the Heceta Head Lighthouse.

Paranormal activity reported in the lighthouse

THE HECETA HEAD LIGHTHOUSE in Oregon is one of the most well-known and picturesque lighthouses in the Pacific Northwest. Built in 1894, it sits atop a 205-foot cliff overlooking the Pacific Ocean, guiding ships safely through the rocky coastline. However, the lighthouse is not only famous for its beauty and practicality but also for its paranormal activity.

The lighthouse was home to several keepers and their families over the years. One of the most famous keepers was the first, William M. Smith, who served from 1894 to 1899. Smith and his wife, Mary, had five children and lived in the small house adjacent to the lighthouse. The family had to endure harsh living conditions, including limited access to fresh water, and they had to haul it up from the beach below. They also had to deal with the constant fog, which meant that William had to sound the foghorn every twenty minutes for hours on end.

There have been many stories of paranormal activity in the lighthouse, including reports of the ghost of a woman who is believed to be Mary Smith. She is said to appear in the house, walking from room to room, and is often seen gazing out the windows towards the sea. Visitors have also reported hearing strange noises, such as footsteps and doors opening and closing, even when no one else is around. Some have also reported feeling a sense of being watched or followed.

In addition to Mary Smith, there have been reports of other ghostly figures at the lighthouse. One of the most commonly reported ghosts is that of a woman in Victorian clothing, who is believed to have died in the nearby woods. Another is the ghost of a sailor who is said to have died in a shipwreck off the coast.

There are several theories as to why the lighthouse may be haunted. Some believe that the harsh living conditions and isolation may have driven the keepers and their families to despair, leading to lingering spirits. Others suggest that the ghosts may be residual energy from past events, such as shipwrecks and deaths that occurred off the coast. Whatever the reason, the paranormal activity at the Heceta Head Lighthouse continues to intrigue and fascinate visitors to this day.

Overall, the history of the Heceta Head Lighthouse and its keepers is rich with tales of hardship and bravery, and the reported paranormal activity adds an extra layer of mystery to this already fascinating location.

Chapter 6: Oregon Caves

The history of the caves and their discovery

The Oregon Caves are a unique geological formation that consists of underground chambers and passages located in southwestern Oregon's Siskiyou Mountains. The caves were formed by the dissolution of marble, a type of metamorphic rock, by groundwater over millions of years. The caves were discovered in 1874 by a local hunter named Elijah Davidson, who stumbled upon the entrance while chasing a bear. The caves have since become a popular tourist destination and a National Monument, attracting thousands of visitors every year.

The discovery of the Oregon Caves was a significant event in the region's history, as it opened up new possibilities for scientific study and tourism. The first explorers to enter the caves were led by a geologist named William J. Melville, who was impressed by the caves' beauty and unique geological formations. Melville recognized the potential for the caves to become a popular tourist attraction, and in 1907, he published a book called "The Oregon Caves and the Rogue River National Forest," which helped to popularise the caves and attract more visitors.

The Oregon Caves are home to a variety of unique geological features, including stalactites, stalagmites, and columns, which have formed over millions of years. The caves also contain underground rivers, lakes, and waterfalls, which have carved out some of the chambers and passages. In addition to their geological importance, the caves also provide habitat for a variety of rare and endangered species, including bats and cave crickets.

The Oregon Caves have played an important role in the region's cultural history as well. The local Native American tribes, including the Takelma and the Shasta, believed that the caves were sacred and used them for spiritual ceremonies. The caves were also used by early pioneers and settlers for shelter and storage, and during the 1920s and 1930s, they were used as a venue for underground dance parties.

Today, the Oregon Caves are a popular destination for tourists and outdoor enthusiasts, attracting visitors from all over the world. Visitors can take guided tours of the caves, explore the surrounding forests and wilderness areas, and learn about the caves' unique geological and cultural history. The caves are also home to a variety of rare and endangered species, which are protected by the National Park Service and other conservation organisations.

The discovery of the Oregon Caves was a significant event in the region's history, opening up new possibilities for scientific study and tourism. The caves have played an important role in the region's cultural history, serving as a site of spiritual significance for local Native American tribes and a venue for underground dance parties during the early 20th century. Today, the Oregon Caves are a popular destination for visitors from all over the world, offering a unique glimpse into the region's geological and cultural history.

Stories of past explorers and visitors

THE OREGON CAVES, LOCATED in the Siskiyou Mountains in Southern Oregon, have been a popular destination for explorers and visitors for over a century. The history of the caves begins with their discovery in 1874 by a young hunter named Elijah Davidson. While pursuing a black bear in the area, Davidson stumbled upon the cave entrance and was amazed by the beauty and wonder inside.

Word of the discovery quickly spread, and soon after, the first official tour of the Oregon Caves was led by a local businessman named Thomas Condon. Condon recognized the unique geological formations within the caves and saw the potential for tourism. He leased the property from the federal government in 1899 and began building trails and infrastructure to allow visitors to explore the caves.

Over the years, the Oregon Caves have attracted many famous visitors, including President Franklin D. Roosevelt and his wife Eleanor, who visited the caves in 1934. The caves have also been used as a filming location for movies and television shows, including the popular series "Lassie."

One of the most famous stories associated with the Oregon Caves is the legend of the "Shasta Treasure." In the early 1900s, a group of treasure hunters claimed to have found a vast fortune of gold and silver inside the caves. However, the story was later revealed to be a hoax, and no treasure was ever found.

Despite the lack of treasure, the Oregon Caves have continued to be a popular tourist destination. In 1909, the federal government declared the caves a national monument, and in 1937, a lodge was built nearby to accommodate visitors.

Today, visitors can take guided tours of the caves and learn about the unique geology and history of the area. The Oregon Caves National Monument and Preserve also offers a variety of outdoor activities, including hiking, fishing, and camping.

The Oregon Caves have a rich history filled with stories of exploration and adventure. From the discovery of the caves by Elijah Davidson to the modern-day tourist destination, the Oregon Caves continue to fascinate visitors from around the world.

Paranormal activity reported in the caves

THE OREGON CAVES NATIONAL Monument is a popular tourist destination located in the Siskiyou Mountains in southern Oregon. The caves are known for their unique geological formations and stunning beauty, but they are also known for their reported paranormal activity.

The history of the Oregon caves dates back millions of years when they were formed by natural forces. The caves were discovered in 1874 by Elijah Davidson, a local hunter, and were later explored and mapped by a team of surveyors in 1909. The caves were officially designated as a National Monument in 1909, making them one of the oldest National Monuments in the United States.

Over the years, the caves have attracted thousands of visitors and explorers, many of whom have reported experiencing paranormal activity. One of the most common reports is the feeling of being watched or followed by an unseen presence. Visitors have reported hearing whispers and voices coming from within the caves, as well as feeling cold spots and sudden drops in temperature.

One of the most famous stories associated with the Oregon caves is the legend of the "Chateau at the End of the Oregon Trail." According to the legend, a group of pioneers settled in the area in the mid-1800s and built a large mansion near the caves. The mansion was said to be haunted by the ghosts of the original settlers, who were rumoured to have died under mysterious circumstances. While there is no evidence to support the existence of the mansion or the deaths of the settlers, the legend persists to this day and has become a popular part of the lore surrounding the caves.

Another reported paranormal phenomenon at the Oregon caves is the presence of orbs in photographs taken within the caves. Orbs are circular or semi-circular shapes that are often believed to be manifestations of spirits or other paranormal entities. While some sceptics attribute orbs to dust, moisture, or other natural phenomena, many visitors to the Oregon caves believe that the orbs they capture in their photographs are evidence of the supernatural.

In addition to orbs, visitors to the Oregon caves have reported seeing apparitions and shadowy figures within the caves. Some have reported feeling as though they are being touched or pushed by unseen hands, while others have reported feeling a sense of dread or foreboding while exploring the caves.

While the reported paranormal activity at the Oregon caves is certainly intriguing, it is important to approach such reports with a healthy dose of scepticism. Many factors can contribute to the perception of paranormal activity, including environmental conditions, suggestibility, and preconceived beliefs. However, for those who are interested in exploring the mysteries of the Oregon caves, there is no shortage of stories and legends to discover, and the caves remain one of the most fascinating and mysterious destinations in the Pacific Northwest.

Chapter 7: Flavel House in Astoria

The history of the Flavel family and their home

The Flavel House, located in Astoria, Oregon, is a historic mansion that was once the residence of one of the most prominent families in the city. The Flavel family played a significant role in the development of Astoria, and their home is now a popular tourist attraction and museum. The history of the Flavel family and their home is a fascinating story that provides insight into the early days of Astoria and the life of a wealthy family in the late 1800s.

The Flavel family was led by Captain George Conrad Flavel, who was born in 1833 in New Hampshire. Flavel moved to Oregon in 1850, where he became a successful entrepreneur and businessman. He invested in real estate, shipping, and fishing, which helped him accumulate a considerable fortune. In 1885, Flavel decided to build a grand mansion for his family, and he hired a prominent architect from Portland to design the home.

The Flavel House was completed in 1886 and was a grand display of wealth and opulence. The home featured Victorian-style architecture, with intricate details and decorations throughout. It was three stories tall and had 11 bedrooms, several sitting rooms, a formal dining room, and a large kitchen. The house also had modern amenities for its time, such as indoor plumbing, gas lighting, and a central heating system.

The Flavel family was known for their lavish lifestyle, and the house was a reflection of that. They held elaborate parties and social events, often inviting guests from all over the world. The family was also involved in many community organisations and philanthropic efforts, which helped them gain respect and admiration from the people of Astoria.

Captain Flavel passed away in 1893, and the house was inherited by his son, George Flavel Jr. George Jr. was also a successful businessman and community leader, and he continued to live in the house with his wife and children. However, the family's wealth began to decline in the early 1900s, and they were forced to sell off some of their properties, including a steamship company and a large portion of their land.

In 1934, the Flavel House was sold to the Episcopal Diocese of Oregon and was used as a rectory for the nearby church. The house was then sold again in 1951 to a local business owner who used it as an office space for his company. However, the house fell into disrepair and was almost demolished in the 1960s.

In 1963, the Clatsop County Historical Society purchased the Flavel House and restored it to its former grandeur. The house was opened to the public as a museum in 1955 and has since become one of Astoria's most popular tourist attractions.

The Flavel House is now listed on the National Register of Historic Places and is a popular destination for history enthusiasts and architecture lovers. The house is open to the public for guided tours, which take visitors through the various rooms and provide insight into the lives of the Flavel family and the history of Astoria.

The Flavel House is not just a grand mansion but also a significant piece of Astoria's history. The story of the Flavel family and their home provides a glimpse into the life of a wealthy family in the late 1800s and early 1900s, as well as the development of Astoria as a city. The house's restoration and transformation into a museum have allowed visitors to appreciate and learn from the past, making the Flavel House an essential part of Oregon's cultural heritage.

Stories of the family and their impact on Astoria

THE FLAVEL FAMILY IS one of the most prominent and influential families in Astoria's history. The family's patriarch, Captain George Flavel, played a significant role in shaping Astoria's development in the late 19th century. George Flavel was born in New Hampshire in 1823 and began his seafaring career at the age of 14. He eventually settled in Astoria in the mid-1850s and became one of the city's leading citizens. He played an important role in Astoria's early development, serving as a city councilman and as a representative in the Oregon State Legislature.

The Flavel family's home in Astoria is one of the city's most well-known and historic buildings. The house was built in 1884 by George Flavel and his wife Mary Christina, and it remained in the Flavel family until 1934. The house was then sold to the

Clatsop County Historical Society, and it was opened to the public as a museum in 1951. The Flavel House Museum has since become one of Astoria's most popular tourist attractions, drawing visitors from all over the world.

The Flavel House is a stunning example of Queen Anne architecture, which was popular in the late 19th century. The house is known for its intricate detailing, including a wrap-around porch, a tower, and stained-glass windows. The house has 11 rooms, each of which is filled with antique furniture and artefacts that provide a glimpse into the Flavel family's life in Astoria.

The Flavel family was known for their lavish lifestyle and their many contributions to Astoria's social and cultural scene. George Flavel was a prominent member of the local Masonic lodge, and his wife Mary was involved in numerous charitable organisations. The Flavels were known for their hospitality, and their home was often the site of lavish parties and social gatherings. The family's influence can still be seen throughout Astoria today, from the Flavel House Museum to the many other historic buildings that they helped to build and maintain.

The Flavel family was also known for their many philanthropic endeavours. They donated large sums of money to various charitable organisations, including hospitals and schools. George Flavel was particularly passionate about education, and he was instrumental in the establishment of the Astoria Public Library. The Flavels also supported the local arts scene, and they were known for their patronage of the Astoria Opera House.

Overall, the Flavel family had a significant impact on the development of Astoria in the late 19th and early 20th centuries. Their home, the Flavel House Museum, is a testament to their legacy and their contributions to the city's cultural and social scene. Visitors to Astoria can still experience the Flavel family's legacy today, whether through a tour of the Flavel House Museum or by exploring the many other historic sites and landmarks that they helped to build and preserve.

Paranormal activity reported in the house

THE FLAVEL HOUSE IN Astoria, Oregon is a well-known historic landmark that was once the home of the influential Flavel family. It was built in 1884 by Captain George Flavel, a prominent businessman, and sea captain. The Flavels were a family of great wealth and social standing in the community, and their legacy can still be seen in Astoria today.

Over the years, many stories have emerged about the Flavel family and their impact on the community. Captain George Flavel was a respected figure in Astoria, and he used his wealth and influence to build schools and churches, and to support other community initiatives. He was also an accomplished seaman, and his knowledge and expertise were highly valued in the maritime community.

Captain Flavel's son, George Conrad Flavel, continued the family legacy of public service, serving as mayor of Astoria for several terms. The family's wealth and social standing allowed them to enjoy a luxurious lifestyle, and their home was a reflection of their status in the community.

In the years since the Flavels lived in the house, many stories have emerged about the family and their impact on Astoria. Some of these stories are tragic, such as the story of Alice Flavel, the captain's daughter, who died at a young age from an illness.

There are also stories of mysterious happenings in the house, with many people reporting unexplained phenomena and strange occurrences. Some people have reported hearing footsteps and voices, even when no one else is around. Others have reported seeing apparitions and strange lights in the house.

One of the most common reports of paranormal activity in the Flavel House is the presence of the ghost of Mary Flavel, the captain's wife. Visitors to the house have reported feeling her presence in various parts of the house, and some have even reported seeing her ghostly figure.

Despite the many stories of paranormal activity in the Flavel House, there are also many who believe that the stories are simply a product of people's imaginations. However, the stories continue to be told, and the Flavel House remains a popular destination for those interested in the history and paranormal activity of the Pacific Northwest.

Chapter 8: The Ashland Springs Hotel

The history of the hotel and its significance to Ashland

The Ashland Springs Hotel is a historic hotel located in Ashland, Oregon. Built in 1925, the hotel has served as a cornerstone of the community for nearly a century. The hotel is situated in the heart of downtown Ashland, just a few blocks from the renowned Oregon Shakespeare Festival. The Ashland Springs Hotel has a long and fascinating history, one that is deeply intertwined with the history of the town.

In the early 20th century, Ashland was a thriving community that was experiencing rapid growth. The town was home to a number of businesses and industries, including timber, agriculture, and mining. As the town grew, so too did the need for quality accommodations. In 1925, local businessman John McCall purchased a parcel of land in downtown Ashland with the intention of building a grand hotel. McCall hired architect Henry Johnstone to design the hotel, which was to be called the Lithia Springs Hotel.

Construction of the hotel began in 1925 and was completed the following year. The Lithia Springs Hotel was a grand, five-story building that featured 70 guest rooms, a grand ballroom, a restaurant, and a rooftop garden. The hotel was built in the popular Renaissance Revival style, which was characterised by grand arches, ornate decorations, and a sense of grandeur.

The Lithia Springs Hotel was an immediate success, drawing guests from all over the country. The hotel quickly became the social hub of the town, hosting dances, concerts, and other events. Over the years, the hotel has hosted a number of notable guests, including President Herbert Hoover, who stayed at the hotel during a visit to Ashland in 1929.

In 1950, the hotel was purchased by the Flanagan family, who renamed it the Ashland Springs Hotel. The Flanagans operated the hotel for over 50 years, during which time they oversaw a number of renovations and improvements. In 2000, the hotel was purchased by Doug and Becky Neuman, who embarked on a major restoration project. The Neumans worked to restore the hotel to its original grandeur, while also adding modern amenities and conveniences.

Today, the Ashland Springs Hotel is a thriving hotel that continues to be a cornerstone of the community. The hotel features 70 guest rooms, a restaurant, a bar, and a number of event spaces. The hotel is also home to the Waterstone Spa, a luxurious spa that offers a variety of treatments and services.

The Ashland Springs Hotel is an important part of Ashland's history, and it continues to play a vital role in the town's social and economic fabric. The hotel is a testament to the town's rich history and vibrant culture, and it remains a popular destination for visitors from all over the world.

Stories of past guests and employees

THE ASHLAND SPRINGS Hotel, located in the heart of Ashland, Oregon, has a long and storied history. Originally built in 1925, it served as a community centre for the town before being converted into a hotel in the 1940s. Over the years, the hotel has hosted countless guests, many of whom have left their mark on the building in one way or another.

One famous guest who stayed at the Ashland Springs Hotel was the famous author John Steinbeck, who wrote part of his novel "East of Eden" during his stay. Other notable guests have included politicians, actors, and musicians, such as Ronald Reagan, Bob Hope, and Tony Bennett.

In addition to its famous guests, the hotel has also seen its fair share of colourful employees over the years. One story tells of a former desk clerk who worked at the hotel for over 30 years and was known for his gruff demeanour and tendency to play practical jokes on guests. Another employee, a former housekeeper, was rumoured to have stayed on as a ghostly presence after her death.

The hotel has also had a number of mysterious and unexplained events occur over the years. Guests and employees alike have reported strange noises, objects moving on their own, and unexplained shadows or apparitions. Some have even reported seeing the ghostly figure of a woman in a long white dress walking the halls of the hotel.

One particularly eerie story involves a group of guests who were staying in one of the hotel's suites. Late at night, they were awoken by the sound of someone walking around in the room above them. Thinking it was simply another guest, they decided to ignore it and try to get back to sleep. However, the footsteps continued, growing louder and more persistent as the night went on. Eventually, the guests could take it no longer and called down to the front desk to complain. The clerk who answered the phone was puzzled, however, as the room above the guests' had been unoccupied for weeks.

Another story involves a former employee who was working late one night in the hotel's basement. As she was going about her work, she suddenly felt a cold breeze and heard the sound of someone breathing behind her. Turning around, she saw the ghostly figure of a man standing just a few feet away. Terrified, she ran up the stairs and out of the basement, vowing never to return.

Despite these spooky tales, the Ashland Springs Hotel remains a popular destination for visitors to Ashland. Its rich history, luxurious accommodations, and beautiful surroundings make it a truly unique and special place to stay.

Paranormal activity reported in the hotel

THE ASHLAND SPRINGS Hotel, located in the charming town of Ashland, Oregon, is a historic landmark that has been welcoming guests since 1925. The hotel has become known not just for its elegant accommodations and excellent service, but also for the paranormal activity that has been reported by guests and employees over the years.

GHOSTS OF OREGON: THE TOP 10 HAUNTED PLACES YOU MUST VISIT

One of the most commonly reported paranormal experiences at the Ashland Springs Hotel is the sighting of a ghostly woman dressed in 1930s attire, wandering the hallways of the hotel. She is believed to be the ghost of an actress who stayed at the hotel during the 1940s and was said to have taken her own life in one of the guest rooms. Her apparition has been seen in several areas of the hotel, including the lobby, the second-floor landing, and the hallway outside of her former room.

In addition to the ghostly woman, guests have reported other unexplainable occurrences, such as doors opening and closing on their own, strange noises in the middle of the night, and sudden drops in temperature in certain areas of the hotel. Some guests have even reported feeling as though they were being watched by an unseen presence.

One of the most famous stories of paranormal activity at the Ashland Springs Hotel involves Room 302. This room is said to be haunted by the ghost of a young girl who died in the hotel in the 1940s. Guests who have stayed in this room have reported feeling a cold breeze or a light touch on their cheek, as though the ghostly girl is trying to communicate with them.

Another room that has been known to be haunted is Room 208. Guests who have stayed in this room have reported strange smells and unexplainable noises, as well as the feeling of being touched by an unseen presence. Some guests have even reported seeing the apparition of a man standing in the room, though his identity remains a mystery.

The hotel's staff has also reported strange occurrences, including hearing footsteps and voices when no one else is around, and feeling as though they are being watched while working in certain areas of the hotel. Some employees have even reported seeing full-bodied apparitions, including the ghostly woman in 1930s attire.

Despite the reported paranormal activity, the Ashland Springs Hotel remains a popular destination for travellers seeking a unique and historical lodging experience. Whether or not you believe in ghosts, a stay at the Ashland Springs Hotel is sure to be a memorable one.

Chapter 9: Hot Lake Hotel

The history of the hotel and its significance to Eastern Oregon

The Hot Lake Hotel is a historic property located in Eastern Oregon, near the city of La Grande. The hotel has a fascinating history that spans over a century, and it has played an important role in the development of the region. The building is a beautiful example of early 20th-century architecture and has been a prominent landmark in the area since its construction in 1908.

The history of the Hot Lake Hotel dates back to the late 19th century when a group of investors led by E. E. Wilson decided to build a sanatorium in the area. The hotel was originally intended to serve as a destination for people seeking treatment for various illnesses, particularly those related to the lungs. At the time, the area was known for its clean air and natural hot springs, which were believed to have healing properties.

Construction of the hotel began in 1903 and was completed in 1908. The building was designed by prominent architect John Virginius Bennes and featured a grand, neoclassical facade with Ionic columns and ornate detailing. The interior of the hotel was just as impressive, with a grand lobby, a luxurious dining room, and spacious guest rooms.

The Hot Lake Hotel quickly became a popular destination for people seeking rest and relaxation. Guests would come from all over the country to enjoy the hotel's hot springs, which were piped into the building and used to heat the water for the hotel's indoor swimming pool. The hotel also featured a spa, a bowling alley, a billiards room, and a large ballroom where guests could dance the night away.

Over the years, the Hot Lake Hotel changed hands several times and underwent a number of renovations. In the 1920s, the hotel was purchased by Dr. F. N. Caldwell, who turned it into a hospital. During this time, the hotel's focus shifted from providing a luxurious retreat to providing medical care to the community. The hospital continued to operate until the 1970s when it was closed due to financial difficulties.

After sitting vacant for many years, the Hot Lake Hotel was purchased by David and Lee Manuel in the 1990s. The couple spent several years restoring the building to its former glory, and today, the Hot Lake Hotel is once again a popular destination for travellers looking for a unique and historic experience.

The Hot Lake Hotel is also known for its paranormal activity, and it has been featured on a number of television shows, including "Ghost Adventures" and "Ghost Hunters." There have been reports of ghostly apparitions, strange noises, and other unexplained phenomena in the hotel, particularly in the old hospital wing of the building.

Overall, the Hot Lake Hotel is a fascinating example of Eastern Oregon's history and is an important part of the region's heritage. Its beautiful architecture, luxurious amenities, and storied past make it a unique and memorable destination for travellers from around the world.

Stories of past guests and employees

THE HOT LAKE HOTEL, located in La Grande, Oregon, has a rich history dating back to the early 20th century. The hotel was originally built as a sanatorium in 1864, catering to people seeking the healing powers of the nearby hot springs. The sanatorium operated for over 40 years, but eventually fell into disrepair.

In 1917, Dr. Phy became the owner of the sanatorium and transformed it into the Hot Lake Hotel. The new hotel quickly became a popular destination for wealthy travellers seeking the hot springs' therapeutic properties. The hotel had luxurious amenities such as a grand ballroom, a 60-foot indoor pool, and a beauty salon.

During the 1920s and 1930s, the hotel became a hub for social activity, hosting large parties and events. However, in 1934, a devastating fire destroyed much of the hotel, and it was rebuilt on a smaller scale.

Despite the fire, the hotel continued to attract guests until it was forced to close in 1939 due to the outbreak of World War II. During the war, the hotel was used as a veteran's hospital, and later as a nursing home. In the 1970s, the hotel was abandoned and left to deteriorate.

In the 1990s, the hotel was purchased and underwent an extensive restoration, bringing it back to its former glory. The restored hotel features 31 guest rooms, each with a unique design and style.

Throughout the hotel's history, there have been numerous reports of paranormal activity. Many guests have reported seeing apparitions, strange noises, and unexplained movements. Some believe that the spirits of former patients and guests still haunt the hotel.

One of the most famous ghost stories associated with the Hot Lake Hotel involves the ghost of a young girl who drowned in the indoor pool during the hotel's early years. Guests have reported hearing her laughter and seeing wet footprints leading to the pool, even though it has been empty for many years.

Another common paranormal experience reported by guests is the feeling of being touched or brushed past by an invisible presence. Some have reported feeling an icy breath on their skin or hearing unexplained whispers in their ear.

The hotel's haunted reputation has made it a popular destination for paranormal investigators and ghost hunters. Many have recorded strange EVP (Electronic Voice Phenomenon) readings and captured unexplained images on film.

Despite its haunted history, the Hot Lake Hotel continues to attract visitors from all over the world. Whether you believe in ghosts or not, the hotel's rich history and stunning architecture make it a must-visit destination for anyone travelling through Eastern Oregon.

Paranormal activity reported in the hotel

THE HOT LAKE HOTEL, located in La Grande, Oregon, has a long and fascinating history that has led to many reported paranormal experiences over the years. Originally built in 1864 as a simple hot springs resort, the property has gone through many iterations over the years, including functioning as a hospital, sanitarium, and a retreat for the wealthy.

The hotel's original purpose was to capitalise on the natural hot springs located on the property. It was a popular spot for people looking to relax and heal in the warm mineral water, which was said to have therapeutic properties. The hotel's popularity grew, and it became a favoured spot for the wealthy to come and unwind.

In 1917, the hotel was converted into a hospital and sanitarium, serving as a medical facility for over 40 years. During this time, it was known as the "Hot Lake Sanatorium" and became a popular destination for people seeking treatment for a variety of ailments, including tuberculosis.

Over the years, the hospital underwent many changes, and in 1959, the property was sold to the state of Oregon and transformed into a nursing home for the elderly. In 1973, the nursing home was closed down, and the building was left abandoned for several years.

In 1985, the hotel was purchased by a couple named Doug and Becky Nelson, who spent years restoring the building to its former glory. The couple also added a new wing to the hotel, which included a restaurant, banquet hall, and spa.

The hotel's long and varied history has led to many reported paranormal experiences over the years. Some of the most common reports include strange noises, apparitions, and unexplained movements. Guests have reported hearing footsteps, doors opening and closing on their own, and feeling as though they are being watched.

One of the most well-known paranormal experiences reported at the Hot Lake Hotel involves a ghostly woman who is said to haunt the building. According to legend, the woman was a patient at the sanitarium who fell in love with her doctor. When her love was unrequited, she committed suicide by jumping from the roof of the building. Many guests have reported seeing her ghostly figure wandering the halls of the hotel, often in the area around room 208, which is said to be the location of her former room.

Another popular story involves the ghost of a nurse who is said to haunt the building. According to legend, the nurse worked at the hospital during its time as a sanitarium and fell in love with one of the patients. When the patient died, the nurse was so heartbroken that she took her own life. Guests have reported seeing her ghostly figure in the hallways of the hotel, often wearing a nurse's uniform.

Despite the many reported paranormal experiences at the Hot Lake Hotel, the property remains a popular destination for visitors looking to relax and unwind. The hotel's unique history, combined with its reported ghostly activity, has made it a favourite spot for paranormal enthusiasts and history buffs alike.

Chapter 10: Oregon State Capitol

The history of the capitol building and its significance to Salem

The Oregon State Capitol is located in the city of Salem and serves as the home of Oregon's government. The current Capitol building was completed in 1938 and is the third building to serve as the seat of Oregon's government. The history of the Oregon State Capitol dates back to the 1850s when Oregon became a state. The first Capitol building was built in 1854 and served as Oregon's statehouse until it burned down in 1855.

After the fire, the state government moved into a new building which was completed in 1876. This building served as the State Capitol for over sixty years before it was deemed structurally unsound and demolished. The current building was designed by Francis Keally and built between 1936 and 1938 at a cost of $2.5 million.

The Oregon State Capitol building is an excellent example of Art Deco architecture, with a unique copper-clad dome that stands 121 feet tall. The dome is topped by a statue called the "Oregon Pioneer" which was created by sculptor Ulric Ellerhusen. The statue is made of aluminium and stands 22 feet tall, weighing 8,000 pounds.

The Oregon State Capitol building is significant not only for its architectural beauty but also for the events that have taken place inside. The building has served as the centre of Oregon's government, witnessing the passage of significant legislation, the inauguration of governors, and the workings of the state's judicial system.

One of the most notable events to take place at the Oregon State Capitol was the Vanport flood in 1948. The flood devastated the city of Vanport, which was located near Portland and had been built to house workers during World War II. The flood killed 15 people and left thousands homeless. Governor Earl Snell declared a state of emergency and established temporary housing at the Oregon State Fairgrounds, which is located near the State Capitol building.

Another significant event that took place at the Oregon State Capitol was the passage of the Beach Bill in 1967. The Beach Bill granted public access to all of Oregon's beaches, making them some of the most accessible and beautiful in the country.

Throughout its history, the Oregon State Capitol building has undergone numerous renovations and restorations. In 1977, the building underwent a major renovation that included the installation of a new heating and cooling system and the removal of asbestos.

In 2019, the Oregon State Capitol building underwent a $120 million renovation that aimed to address issues with seismic safety, accessibility, and the ageing mechanical systems. The renovation project included the restoration of the Capitol's iconic rotunda, the addition of a new underground parking garage, and the installation of new security measures.

Today, the Oregon State Capitol building remains an important symbol of the state's government and history. Visitors can take guided tours of the building, visit the state's legislative chambers, and explore the many exhibits that showcase Oregon's rich cultural and natural heritage.

Stories of past politicians and employees

THE OREGON STATE CAPITOL Building is a grand structure located in Salem, the capital city of Oregon. It is the heart of the Oregon Legislature and has served as the centre of the state government since 1938. The Capitol is not just a government building; it is also a symbol of the state's political and cultural identity. Over the years, the Capitol has seen many politicians come and go, and with them, some fascinating stories.

One of the most notable politicians to have worked in the Capitol building was Governor Tom McCall. McCall was a popular governor in the state and is remembered for his environmental activism. He was instrumental in the establishment of the state's bottle bill, which was the first of its kind in the nation. During his tenure as governor from 1967-1975, he was also responsible for the removal of the Harbor Drive freeway in Portland and the establishment of the Oregon Coastal Conservation and Development Commission.

Another prominent figure in the history of the Capitol is former Oregon Secretary of State, Barbara Roberts. She served in the role from 1985-1995 and was the first woman to be elected to statewide office in Oregon. Roberts was known for her work on environmental and education issues and is remembered as a trailblazer for women in politics.

The Oregon Capitol has also been home to many dedicated employees over the years. One of the most notable was Doris Penwell, who worked as a legislative secretary for over 30 years. She was known for her dedication and efficiency, and her legacy lives on in the Doris Penwell Memorial Reading Room, located on the second floor of the Capitol.

The Capitol has also seen its share of controversy over the years. In 1984, a group of armed militants calling themselves the "Republic of Oregon" took over the Capitol building in protest of federal land-use policies. The standoff lasted for 10 days before the militants finally surrendered. This incident remains a fascinating and controversial event in the history of the Capitol.

In addition to the political figures and employees who have worked in the Capitol, there are also stories of paranormal activity within the building. Many visitors and staff members have reported strange occurrences, including unexplained noises, doors opening and closing on their own, and sightings of apparitions.

One of the most well-known ghost stories associated with the Capitol involves the ghost of Governor Oswald West. West served as governor from 1911-1915 and is said to haunt the building to this day. Visitors and staff members have reported seeing his ghostly figure walking the halls of the Capitol or standing in front of his portrait in the governor's office.

Another ghostly presence that has been reported in the Capitol is that of a woman in a long, flowing dress. Some believe this may be the ghost of Marion Jack, a young woman who worked in the building during the 1930s and is said to have died tragically in the building. Others believe the woman in the dress may be the ghost of another former employee or even the ghost of a visitor who died in the building.

Overall, the Oregon State Capitol building has a rich history filled with fascinating stories of politicians, employees, and even ghosts. As the centre of Oregon's political and cultural identity, it will continue to play an important role in the state's future, while also preserving its unique past.

Paranormal activity reported in the building

THE OREGON STATE CAPITOL building, located in Salem, Oregon, is not only the centre of the state's government, but it also has a rich history that dates back to its construction in 1935. Over the years, there have been many reports of paranormal activity within the building, making it a popular destination for ghost hunters and those interested in the supernatural.

The history of the Oregon State Capitol building begins in the early 1900s when the original Capitol building was deemed too small for the growing government. A new building was proposed and construction began in 1936. However, construction was delayed due to budget cuts during the Great Depression, and it wasn't until 1938 that the building was finally completed.

Over the years, the Capitol building has seen many politicians and employees come and go, and with them have come stories of paranormal activity. One of the most commonly reported sightings is that of a young girl who is said to haunt the building. Many believe she is the ghost of a girl who died in the building during its construction. She is said to appear as a misty figure in the rotunda and has been seen by numerous employees and visitors.

Another common sighting is that of a ghostly figure who is seen in the basement of the building. The figure is said to be a former janitor who worked in the building and died in the 1950s. He is often seen in the basement, and some have reported hearing strange noises and footsteps coming from the area.

There have also been reports of other strange occurrences within the building. Some have reported hearing voices and footsteps when no one else is around, while others have reported objects moving on their own. Some have even reported seeing apparitions in the hallways.

These reports of paranormal activity have led many to believe that the Capitol building is haunted by the ghosts of those who have passed through its halls over the years. Some believe that the spirits are restless and are trying to communicate with the living, while others believe they are simply residual energy left over from past events.

GHOSTS OF OREGON: THE TOP 10 HAUNTED PLACES YOU MUST VISIT

Despite the reports of paranormal activity, the Oregon State Capitol building remains a popular destination for visitors and politicians alike. In fact, many have reported feeling a sense of history and significance when they enter the building, as if the spirits of those who came before them are still watching over the building and its occupants.

Overall, the Oregon State Capitol building is a fascinating piece of Oregon's history, both in terms of its government and its paranormal activity. While the stories of ghosts and other supernatural occurrences may be difficult to prove, they continue to add to the building's allure and mystery. Whether you are a believer or a sceptic, a visit to the Oregon State Capitol building is sure to leave an impression on all who enter its doors.

EDWARD TURNER

Conclusion

Oregon has a rich history of ghost stories and paranormal activity, with numerous places around the state being known for their eerie past and unexplained occurrences. Here are the top 10 most haunted places in Oregon, based on their historical significance, reported paranormal activity, and popularity among locals and tourists alike.

1. Shanghai Tunnels, Portland: The Shanghai Tunnels are a network of underground passages that were used to transport goods and people in the late 19th century. However, they also had a dark side, as they were used to kidnap and sell men as forced labourers to work on ships. The tunnels are said to be haunted by the spirits of those who suffered and died there, with reports of disembodied voices, apparitions, and strange sounds.

2. McMenamins White Eagle Saloon, Portland: This historic saloon was once a popular spot for sailors and loggers, and is said to be haunted by the ghost of a former prostitute named Rose, who was murdered on the premises. Visitors have reported strange noises, sudden temperature drops, and the feeling of being watched by unseen entities.

3. Geiser Grand Hotel, Baker City: Built in 1889 during the Gold Rush, the Geiser Grand Hotel is a beautiful Victorian-era building that has hosted many famous guests over the years. However, it is also said to be home to several ghosts, including

a former maid named Alice, who has been seen wandering the halls and disappearing into thin air.

4. Oregon State Hospital, Salem: The Oregon State Hospital was established in 1883 as a treatment centre for the mentally ill, but became infamous for its cruel and inhumane practices. The hospital has since been renovated, but is still said to be haunted by the spirits of former patients and staff, with reports of strange noises, shadowy figures, and unexplained phenomena.

5. Heceta Head Lighthouse, Florence: Located on a rocky promontory overlooking the Pacific Ocean, the Heceta Head Lighthouse has been in operation since 1894. However, it is also said to be haunted by the ghost of a former keeper named Rue, who died in a tragic accident in the early 20th century. Visitors have reported strange noises, mysterious footsteps, and unexplained lights.

6. Oregon Caves, Cave Junction: The Oregon Caves are a series of natural limestone caverns that were discovered in 1874. While they are a popular tourist attraction, they are also said to be haunted by the ghosts of past explorers and Native Americans, with reports of strange noises, apparitions, and unexplained sensations.

7. Flavel House Museum, Astoria: The Flavel House Museum is a beautiful Victorian-era home that was built in 1885 for one of Astoria's most prominent families. However, it is also said to be haunted by the ghosts of the Flavel family themselves, with reports of strange sounds, eerie apparitions, and unexplained activity.

GHOSTS OF OREGON: THE TOP 10 HAUNTED PLACES YOU MUST VISIT

8. Ashland Springs Hotel, Ashland: Built in 1925, the Ashland Springs Hotel is a stunning example of Art Deco architecture and has hosted many famous guests over the years. However, it is also said to be haunted by several ghosts, including a former maid named Flo, who has been seen wandering the halls and playing pranks on guests.

9. Hot Lake Hotel, La Grande: The Hot Lake Hotel is a historic building that was originally built in 1864 as a health spa. However, it is also said to be haunted by the ghosts of past guests and employees, with reports of strange sounds, eerie apparitions, and unexplained sensations.

10. Oregon State Capitol Building, Salem: The Oregon State Capitol Building is the seat of the state government and was built in 1939 in a beautiful Art Deco style. However, it is also said to be haunted by the spirits of former politicians and employees, with reports of strange noises, unexplained footsteps, and apparitions. One of the most famous ghost stories is that of the Lady in Blue, who is said to be the ghost of a woman who died in a construction accident during the building's construction. Visitors and employees have reported seeing her ghostly figure in the halls and hearing her weeping.

Overall, Oregon has a rich history of haunted places that attract both sceptics and believers alike. While the stories may vary in their authenticity, there is no denying the eerie atmosphere and unexplained occurrences that make these places so fascinating to explore. Whether you're a paranormal enthusiast or simply looking for a spooky adventure, these top 10 haunted places in Oregon are sure to send chills down your spine.

For those interested in exploring Oregon's paranormal history further, there are many places to visit and stories to uncover. Here are some recommendations for further exploration:

1. Ghost tours: Many cities in Oregon offer ghost tours that take visitors to some of the most haunted locations in the area. These tours provide a unique way to learn about the history and legends of each location while experiencing the paranormal activity firsthand. Some popular ghost tours in Oregon include the Shanghai Tunnels tour in Portland, the Ghosts of McMinnville tour, and the Haunted History tour in Eugene.

2. Paranormal investigations: For those interested in conducting their own paranormal investigations, there are many groups and organisations in Oregon that offer guided investigations of haunted locations. These investigations provide an opportunity to use specialised equipment and techniques to capture evidence of paranormal activity. Some of the groups that offer paranormal investigations in Oregon include Pacific Northwest Paranormal, Oregon Paranormal Society, and Eugene Paranormal Society.

3. Historical societies and museums: Many historical societies and museums in Oregon have exhibits and archives related to the paranormal history of the state. These resources provide a wealth of information on the legends and stories of each location and can help visitors better understand the historical context of reported paranormal activity. Some examples of historical societies and museums with paranormal exhibits include the Baker Heritage Museum in Baker City, the Oregon Historical Society in Portland, and the Astoria Heritage Museum in Astoria.

4. Books and media: There are many books, documentaries, and podcasts that explore the paranormal history of Oregon. These resources provide in-depth information on the stories and legends of each location, as well as interviews with witnesses and experts. Some popular books on Oregon's paranormal history include "Ghosts of Oregon" by Adam Woog, "Haunted Salem, Oregon" by Tim King, and "Weird Oregon" by Al Eufrasio and Jefferson Davis.

5. Conferences and events: There are several conferences and events held throughout the year in Oregon that focus on the paranormal and supernatural. These events provide an opportunity to hear from experts in the field, attend lectures and workshops, and meet others who share an interest in the paranormal. Some popular events in Oregon include the Oregon Ghost Conference, the Oregon Bigfoot Festival, and the Northwest Paranormal and UFO Conference.

6. Online resources: There are many online resources available for those interested in exploring Oregon's paranormal history. These include websites and blogs dedicated to the subject, online forums and discussion groups, and social media groups focused on the paranormal. Some popular online resources for exploring Oregon's paranormal history include Oregon Haunted Houses, Oregon Paranormal, and Pacific Northwest Haunts.

There are many ways to explore Oregon's rich paranormal history. Whether through ghost tours, paranormal investigations, historical societies and museums, books and media, conferences and events, or online resources, there is no shortage of opportunities to learn about and experience the supernatural in Oregon. With its long history and diverse landscape, Oregon is sure to continue to fascinate and intrigue those interested in the paranormal for years to come.

Don't miss out!

Visit the website below and you can sign up to receive emails whenever Edward Turner publishes a new book. There's no charge and no obligation.

https://books2read.com/r/B-A-SYIZ-JTKLC

BOOKS 2 READ

Connecting independent readers to independent writers.

Also by Edward Turner

Ghosts of Paris: Ten Haunted Places in the City of Love
Appalachian Nightmares: The Top 10 Creepy Creatures of the Mountains
Asia's Top Ten Cryptids: Legends, Sightings, and Theories
Beyond the Shadows: Unlocking the Mystery of Bigfoot
Evil Women in History: Uncovering the Gruesome Crimes of Ten Notorious Female Killers
Ghosts of London: Ten Haunted Places in The City
Ghosts of New York: Ten Haunted Places in The Big Apple
Ghosts of Oregon: The Top 10 Haunted Places You Must Visit
Ghosts of the Stage: Ten Hauntings at the Theatre
Missouri Nightmares: The Top 10 Chilling Legends
Mothman Unleashed: Into the Darkened Skies
North America's Top Ten Cryptids: Legends, Sightings, and Theories
Philly's Phantom Encounters: Exploring the City's Most Haunted Places
Secrets of the Deep: The Mystery of the Loch Ness Monster
Unsolved Mysteries: Delving into the Shadows of Infamous Murders and Enigmatic Killers
Unveiling the Shadows: A Journey into Financial Crimes and Scandals

About the Author

Edward Turner is a renowned author who specializes in exploring the realms of ghosts, the paranormal, and cryptids. With a captivating writing style and an insatiable curiosity for the unknown, Turner has garnered a dedicated following of readers who are captivated by his thrilling and eerie tales.

Born with an innate fascination for the supernatural, Turner has spent decades delving into the depths of paranormal phenomena, unearthing captivating stories and untangling mysteries that lie beyond the veil of the ordinary. His extensive research and meticulous attention to detail have earned him a reputation as a leading authority in the field.

Through his books, Turner expertly weaves together chilling accounts of encounters with ghosts, offering readers a glimpse into the ethereal world that coexists alongside our own. His ability to paint vivid portraits of spectral apparitions and convey the haunting atmosphere of haunted locations has made his works both spine-tingling and thought-provoking.

Turner's exploration of the paranormal doesn't stop at ghosts. He also dives into the fascinating world of cryptids—creatures that defy conventional explanation. His in-depth investigations into legendary creatures such as Bigfoot, the Loch Ness Monster, and the Chupacabra showcase his commitment to shedding light on these enigmatic beings.

With each page, Edward Turner's readers are drawn deeper into the enigmatic and unknown. His unique storytelling ability combined with his meticulous research has made him a sought-after author for those with an insatiable thirst for the supernatural. Whether delving into ghostly encounters or unraveling the mysteries of elusive cryptids, Turner's books offer a spine-chilling and immersive reading experience that leaves readers questioning the boundaries of our reality.

Edward Turner's works have earned critical acclaim and numerous accolades within the paranormal genre. He continues to explore the unexplained, captivating readers with his distinctive narrative style and unwavering dedication to unveiling the mysteries that lie hidden in the shadows.

www.ingramcontent.com/pod-product-compliance
Lightning Source LLC
Chambersburg PA
CBHW071357130726
47996CB00002B/966